Contents

Any words appearing in bold, **like this**, are explained in the Glossary.

About the experiments and demonstrations

In each chapter of this book you will find a section called 'Science Answers'. This describes an experiment or demonstration that you can try yourself. There are some simple safety rules to follow when doing an experiment:

- Ask an adult to help with any cutting using a sharp knife.
- Mains electricity is dangerous. Never, ever try to experiment with it.
- Do not use any of your experimental materials near a mains electrical socket.

Materials you will use

Most of the experiments and demonstrations in this book can be done with objects that you can find in your own home. A few will need items that you can buy from a hardware shop. You will also need paper and pencil to record your results.

What are materials?

Materials are what things are made from. We use different materials to make different things.

Some common materials are stone, wood, glass, cotton and china. Think about one of these materials. Can you write a list of words to describe what it is like? For glass, you might choose breakable, hard, **waterproof** and **transparent**. We call these the **properties** of the material.

Materials all around us

Every day you use things made of many different materials. You might use a toothbrush made from plastic, a shirt made from cotton, a jumper made from wool, a plate made from china, a spoon made from metal, a chair made from wood, a lunchbox made from plastic and a window made from glass. A different material has been used to make each of these things.

Using metals

Gold, silver, copper, aluminium and iron are all metals. They are all alike in some ways: they are strong, they can be polished, they can be shaped and they can be sharpened. Metals can be used to make knives and forks, suits of armour, jewellery, bicycle wheels – and many more things.

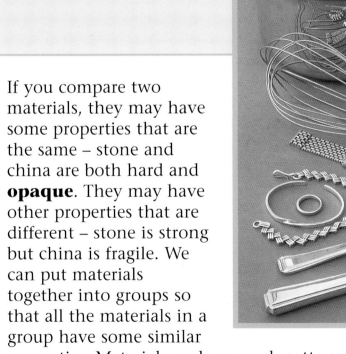

If you compare two materials, they may have some properties that are the same – stone and china are both hard and **opaque**. They may have other properties that are different – stone is strong but china is fragile. We can put materials together into groups so that all the materials in a group have some similar properties. Materials such as wool, cotton, polyester and nylon can all be made into **fabrics.** These are all **flexible** and can be cut, stitched and dyed to make a complete range of different clothes. Slate, marble, granite and chalk are all types of stone. Teak, pine, mahogany and balsa are all types of wood.

Where do materials come from?

Some **materials** come from under the ground, some come from animals and some from plants. These are all natural materials. Some natural materials can be changed to make other materials.

Which materials do we get from the ground?

Some materials are buried a long way below the Earth's surface and have to be dug out from deep mines. Others are near the surface of the Earth and can be dug out more easily.

Many different types of stone can be dug out from hillsides. Stone is used for building. It can also be used for other things like statues and gravestones.

Metals are usually found mixed with other things. These mixtures are called **ores**. Gold is unusual because it is not mixed with other things. It is found in pure lumps called **nuggets**.

Gemstones

Gemstones such as diamonds, rubies, sapphires and emeralds are dug out of the ground too. They are found as rough lumps that are cut and polished so that they sparkle in our jewellery.

Woolly coats

Sheep and some other animals like goats have thick coats of wool. When sheep are **sheared**, the wool is collected and spun into threads. These coats of wool can be woven into a soft, warm fabric.

Which materials do we get from animals?

Animals provide some very useful and important materials.

Silkworms spin fine threads of silk to make their cocoons. We can weave these threads into a beautiful, soft **fabric**.

Leather comes from the skins of animals such as cows. The skins are treated with special chemicals and may be dyed to change the colour. Leather can be used to make soft, **flexible** shoes, jackets, bags and other things.

Bones, horns and tusks have been used by people for thousands of years. They have been made into musical instruments, ornaments, tools, weapons and many, many other things.

Which materials do we get from plants?

When trees are cut down, the wood from the trunks and branches can be used for building, or for making furniture, musical instruments, ornaments and many other things.

Hairy seed pods from cotton bushes can be collected, and the **fibres** inside can be cleaned and spun into cotton threads. We use these threads to make fabrics. Threads from the flax plant are spun and woven to make linen.

Some plants like willow have long thin branches that can be cut and dried. These are called canes and can be used to make baskets and furniture.

Many plants have brightly coloured flowers, leaves and berries. These can be squashed and the juice that oozes out can be collected. From this, we can make many dyes that we use to colour things.

Rubber trees

Rubber trees produce a sticky juice called **sap**. This can be collected and used to make bouncy balls, car tyres and elastic.

DEMONSTRATION: How to make your own material dye.

You can collect your own dye and colour a piece of material by following the steps below.

EQUIPMENT:

Some berries (check with an adult before you choose your berries – some are poisonous. Blackberries, blueberries, raspberries and strawberries are all good to use), two plastic bowls, thin material such as cheesecloth or muslin, an elastic band, a white handkerchief or scrap piece of material and a potato masher or fork.

DEMONSTRATION STEPS:

1 Put your berries in one of the bowls.
2 Squash and mash them until they are completely broken into a pulp. (If it is really dry, you may need to add a little water.)
3 Fix your material over the top of the other bowl with the elastic band so that it is loosely covered.
4 Carefully, pour your pulp into the material and let it drip through into the bowl.
5 Throw away the material and pulp.
6 The bowl should contain a coloured liquid.
7 Dip your material into the liquid, then allow it to dry.
8 Rinse it under the tap. Does the colour rinse away?
9 Write down what you saw.

EXPLANATION:

We can make natural dyes from berries.

How are materials made?

Many of the **materials** around us have been made by changing natural materials into something else. These new materials are called man-made or **manufactured** materials. Some manufactured materials are paper, glass, plastic and paint.

How is paper made?

Paper is made from wood. Trees are chopped down and the trunks are transported to a saw mill. The trunks are sawn into tiny pieces and then mixed with chemicals to make a slush called pulp. Sometimes, **bleach** is mixed with the pulp to make it white. Then the pulp is poured on to a flat screen like a giant sieve to let the water drain out. The pulp is pressed to squash out any water that is left, and then dried. When the paper is removed from the screen it is ready to be cut into smaller pieces ready for use.

How is glass made?

Glass is made from two basic materials – sand and limestone. When these are heated together, they change and make a new material that we know as glass. Bottles, vases and ornaments can be shaped by blowing air into the hot, molten glass. Sometimes, other materials are added to the mixture to make special types of glass. Lead may be added to make fine glass for wine glasses. Other chemicals can be added to make coloured glass, or to make the glass stronger or heatproof.

Can we make new metals?

Mixing two or more metals together can make a new metallic material called an alloy. Brass is made by mixing copper and zinc. It looks like gold but is much cheaper. Mixing aluminium with other metals produces light, strong alloys that are ideal for making bicycle frames and aeroplane bodies. Adding other metals to steel can make even stronger alloys that are used to make tools such as hammers, spanners and screwdrivers.

Where does plastic come from?

Nearly every plastic is made from chemicals that we get originally from oil. At an oil refinery, oil is separated into lots of different chemicals. The chemicals needed to make plastics are removed.

Some plastics can be pulled into long, thin threads and woven into **fabrics** for clothes. They can also be used to make strong ropes, yacht sails and parachutes.

Some plastics can be stretched into very thin sheets to make cling film and other plastic wrappings.

Plastics all around

Dyes can be added to plastics to make every colour of the rainbow! Some plastics can be moulded into shapes to make things like toys and garden furniture. Air can be used to blow them into special shapes to make bottles for drinks and other liquids.

DEMONSTRATION: Make your own plastic.

You can make a plastic material from milk by following the steps below.

EQUIPMENT:

One cup of full fat milk or cream, four to five tablespoons of vinegar, a saucepan or microwave bowl, a spare plastic bowl, a piece of muslin or cheesecloth material, a spoon for stirring and a cooker or microwave oven.

DEMONSTRATION STEPS:

1 Ask an adult to help you to pour the milk into the saucepan or microwave bowl and heat it gently.
2 When it is hot, but not boiling, add the vinegar.
3 Stir the mixture well – it should start to go thick and lumpy.
4 Leave it to cool for a few minutes.
5 Stretch the material over the other plastic bowl and pour the warm mixture onto it. The liquid should drip through into the bowl.
6 Squeeze all the rubbery material left behind into a ball.
7 Wash the ball under a cold tap.
8 Leave it to dry for a couple of days – then you'll have a ball of your own home-made plastic!
9 Write down what you saw.

EXPLANATION:

The vinegar reacted with a substance in the milk called casein. This type of plastic is used to manufacture many products including buttons, beads and jewellery.

13

Why do we choose certain materials?

When we want to choose a **material** to make something, we need to think about the **properties** it must have, such as its hardness, strength, stretchiness, **transparency**, **flexibility**, ability to be **waterproof** … and lots more.

Hard or soft ?

For some things we need to use a hard material but for other things we need a soft material. Look at the furniture in your house. A desk needs to be hard so that you can put things on it. Wood, metal and some plastics are all hard so they are all good materials to make a desk from. A cushion needs to be soft so that it is comfortable to sit on. **Foam** and feathers are both soft so they are good materials to fill a cushion with.

Does it carry electricity?

Electricity can travel through some materials but not others. Materials that electricity can travel through are called electrical **conductors**. Materials that electricity cannot travel through are called electrical **insulators**. Metals and some ceramics are good electrical conductors. These are used for the centres of electric cables, to carry the electricity from one place to another. Plastics are good electrical insulators. They are used for the outside of cables, plugs and sockets to prevent the electricity leaving the metal centre and causing damage or injury.

Flexible or rigid?

Can you imagine how uncomfortable you would be if all your clothes were stiff? Old suits of armour were made of metal but they needed lots of joints so that the wearer could move around. We need to use **flexible** materials such as **fabric** and some plastics for anything that needs to bend and change its shape, like clothes. Other things such as walls and doors, bridges, bicycles and aeroplanes need to be made from **rigid** materials such as stones, concrete and metal so that they do not bend.

INVESTIGATION: Find out if some elastic bands stretch more than others.

EQUIPMENT:
A selection of elastic bands (some bands should be twice as long as others), a 30 cm ruler, a paper clip and an object, such as a pencil case, that you can hang on to the paper clip.

INVESTIGATION STEPS:
1 Hold your ruler vertically with 0 at the bottom.
2 Slide the paper clip onto the bottom of the elastic band.
3 Attach your object to the paper clip.
4 Hold the top of the first elastic band so that the paper clip is at 0.
5 Write the number that the top of the band reaches to find the number of centimetres the elastic band stretched.
8 Write down your results.
9 Repeat for all your bands.

CONCLUSION:
Some elastic bands stretch more than others.

Can you see a pattern in your results? Do thick bands stretch more than thin ones? Do long ones stretch more than short ones?

When do we need strong materials?

If you see a house being built, you'll see some strong **materials** being used. Walls are often built of stone or brick, as they are very strong materials and can support the weight of the roof and the rest of the building. Another strong material often used for building homes is wood. Other structures such as bridges and skyscrapers also have to be strong. These are often built using a strong steel framework covered with large concrete panels.

Protective materials

We wear protective clothing like bicycle helmets to avoid injuring ourselves. These have to be strong enough to stand up to a severe blow and yet light enough to wear comfortably. Most protective clothing like this is made of some type of plastic.

Cars and other vehicles need to be strong, too, to form a protective case around us when we travel. Most car bodies and aeroplanes are made of specially strengthened metals.

EXPERIMENT: Which types of paper are stronger than others?

HYPOTHESIS:
Thicker, heavier paper will be stronger than thinner paper.

EQUIPMENT:
Strips of different types of paper (such as tissue paper, kitchen paper, writing paper, parcel paper, crêpe paper, wrapping paper), sticky tape, a small plastic bucket or pot with handle (you could use a large yoghurt pot with a handle made from string or wire) and some weights (you could use wooden beads or plastic building blocks, but they must all be the same size).

EXPERIMENT STEPS:
1 Cut strips of paper that are 2 cm wide and 10 cm long.
2 Fold the end of the first strip around the handle of the bucket and stick it in place with the sticky tape.
3 Hold your paper up and carefully add the weights one at a time.
4 Record how many weights the paper held before it snapped.
5 Repeat with each of the other types of paper.

CONCLUSION:
Some types of paper are stronger than others. Can you see a pattern in your results? Are thick papers stronger than thinner ones?

When is waterproofing important?

It is important that things that have to keep water in, like buckets, baths and bottles are all **waterproof**. Many **materials** are waterproof and can be used for these things. Metals and pottery were used for many years, but plastic is becoming more and more common as it is cheaper, easier to **mould** and can be made in a wide range of colours.

Warm and dry

Other things that need to be waterproof are those that have to keep water out, like cagoules, umbrellas and Wellington boots. Some are made of plastic, or **fabric** that has been coated with plastic. Some special materials, like Gore-Tex, have been developed for waterproof clothing. These let water vapour escape, so you do not get hot and sweaty, but they do not let water in. So, you stay dry and comfortable.

EXPERIMENT: Which material is most waterproof?

HYPOTHESIS:
Plastic materials will be more waterproof than fabrics and papers.

EQUIPMENT:
Water, an eyedropper, pipette or drinking straw, a plastic container, an elastic band, a stopwatch or watch with a second hand and different materials to test – polythene, fabric, brown paper and tissue paper.

EXPERIMENT STEPS:
1 Cut a piece of each material bigger than the top of the container.
2 Put the first piece over the top of the container and hold it in place with the elastic band.
3 Carefully add five drops of water to the centre of the material.
4 Time how long it takes for the water to go through the material and into the container.
5 Record your results.
6 Repeat for the next material.

CONCLUSION:
Polythene and other kinds of plastic are completely waterproof – the water just sits on the surface. Some materials, like cotton fabrics soak up some of the water, other materials let the water pass through.

Why do some materials keep you warmer than others?

Heat can pass through some **materials** more easily than it can pass through others. Materials that heat passes through easily are called heat **conductors**. Materials that heat cannot pass through easily are called heat **insulators**.

Trapping heat in our homes

Building materials like brick, wood and glass are good heat conductors. This means that in the winter, heat will be lost from inside a house! To keep the heat trapped inside, we need to use heat insulators. Air is a good heat insulator, so double glazing helps to keep the house warm by putting a barrier of air between the layers of glass.

New houses often have a layer of thick padding between two brick layers, to trap the heat. Older houses can have a plastic foam squirted between the brick layers – it expands and fills the **cavity**, trapping the heat inside the building.

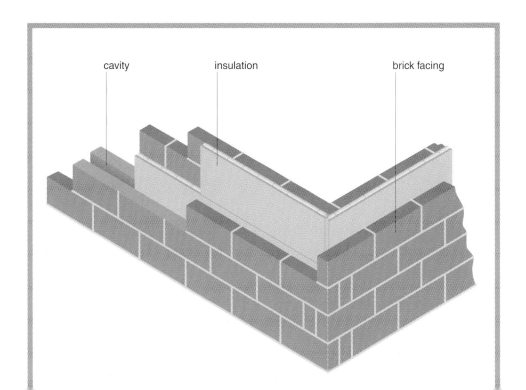

cavity   insulation   brick facing

Keeping our bodies warm

We need to keep our bodies warm too. Air is a good heat insulator, so you often feel warmer with several thin layers of clothes – like a vest, T-shirt and jumper – than you do in one very thick jumper, because air gets trapped between the layers.

Some clothes, like ski suits, are made up of several layers. An outer **waterproof** layer stops water getting in. Below this is a space that traps air, and at the centre is a thick layer of padding that is a good heat insulator. Next comes another space for air, and an inner lining layer of cotton for comfort. Really snug!

Cool picnics

Heat insulators prevent heat passing through them in both directions – so they are good at keeping things cold, too. The same sort of layered structure is used to make cool-bags for picnics and carrying frozen food home from the shops.

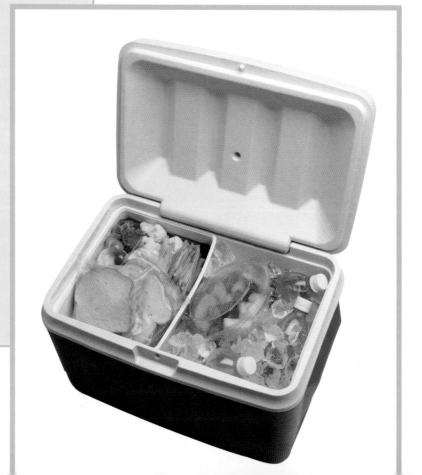

EXPERIMENT: Which material is the best heat insulator?

HYPOTHESIS:

The best heat insulators are those materials that can trap air, because air is a good insulator.

EQUIPMENT:

Hot water (ask an adult to help you with this), a thermometer, some different materials for testing – towel, aluminium foil, bubble wrap, kitchen paper, four identical plastic containers and some elastic bands.

EXPERIMENT STEPS:

1 Wrap each container in one layer of one of your materials. Hold it in place with an elastic band.
2 Measure the temperature of your hot water.
3 Half-fill each container with hot water.
4 Leave the containers for 15 minutes.
5 Measure the temperature of the water in each container.
6 Write down your results.
7 Take each number away from the starting temperature to find out the drop in temperature in each container.

CONCLUSION:

Some materials are better heat insulators than others. The best heat insulator is the material that has the smallest drop in temperature.

What kinds of materials are rocks and soils?

The surface of our planet is made of rock. In many places, the rock is covered by soil or by water so you cannot see it. There are many different types of rock, made in different ways.

Some rocks, like chalk and limestone, were made from the shells and bones of sea creatures that died millions and millions of years ago. These shells and bones were crushed together under the sea and buried beneath many layers of mud.

These rocks are sometimes changed by being heated and crushed below the surface of the Earth. New rocks are formed that are different from the original ones. Marble is formed in this way from limestone.

Some rocks were formed below the surface of the Earth, where it is so hot that the rocks melt. As this molten rock rises to the surface, it cools and forms very hard rock like granite. If it reaches the surface very quickly, perhaps when a volcano erupts, bubbles of gas get trapped inside. The gas bubbles create holes in the molten rock. This is how 'holey' rock, such as pumice, is formed.

We use rocks and stones for many of our buildings and
other structures. If you look at an old building, you may
see signs that it has been damaged over the years. Rocks
can be damaged by the weather and other processes. We
call this damage **weathering**.

Weathering rock

Weathering does not just happen to rocks that we use
for our buildings – it happens to bare rocks on hills and
mountains, sea cliffs and deserts too. Underground caves
are carved out of rocks as water drips through and wears
them away.

What does soil contain?

Soil contains a mixture of different things. The biggest bits are usually small pieces of rocks and pebbles. Then there are tiny pieces of broken-down rock, called clay, and often grains of sand. Most soils contain bits of dead plants and animals, and animal droppings. When this dead **material** breaks down it is called **humus**, and it contains lots of chemicals that plants need to grow well. **Micro-organisms** help to break up the humus and release the chemicals. Some small creatures, like worms and beetles, live in soil too.

Looking at soil

You can see what is in soil by taking some and putting it in a jar with some water. If it is shaken and then left to stand it will slowly settle down into separate layers.

EXPERIMENT: Why does water drain more quickly through some soils than others?

HYPOTHESIS:

Soils with humus and other bits of matter will allow water to drain more quickly than soils without humus.

EQUIPMENT:

Soil samples from different places, such as from under a tree, near a pond, flowerbed, potting compost (ask an adult before you dig!), a plastic scoop or spoon, a funnel, filter paper or cotton wool, a plastic container, water, a measuring jug and a stopwatch or watch with a second hand.

EXPERIMENT STEPS:

1 Set up your filter funnel and paper and stand it in the container.
2 Add the first soil to your filter (count how many scoopfuls you put in).
3 Add water to the top of your soil (measure how much you put in).
4 Wait until the water stops dripping through the funnel into the container.
5 Record how long it took for the water to drain through.
6 Repeat with the next soil.

CONCLUSION:

Water does drain more quickly through some soils than others. Usually soils with a lot of humus will drain more quickly than soils that contain only a little humus.

People who found the answers

Charles Goodyear (1800-1860)

Charles Goodyear, an American inventor, wanted to find a way of treating rubber so that it would not be sticky when hot and hard when cold. In 1839, he accidentally spilt a mixture of rubber and sulphur onto a hot stove – and this gave him a clue about how to improve the rubber. He had discovered that adding sulphur made the rubber stronger. He called his new process 'vulcanization'. It was very successful and is still used for treating rubber today.

Leo Baekeland (1863-1944)

Leo Baekeland was a Belgian scientist who lived in America. He wanted to make a new type of plastic, and eventually managed to develop a plastic he called Bakelite. This was the first 'thermosetting' plastic – it was soft and could be **moulded** when hot, but once set it would not change shape if it was reheated. It became very popular and was soon used to make many household things like door handles, telephones and radios. Bakelite could be made in many colours, and so it was also used to make a lot of jewellery – because many people now collect Bakelite jewellery, it has become very valuable.

Amazing facts

- Diamonds are made from the same stuff as the graphite in many pencil leads! They are both made of a chemical called carbon. All that is different between the two materials is the way the tiny carbon particles are held together.

- Do you have a fleece to keep you warm in cold weather? Can you guess what it is made from? Well, believe it or not, it's probably made from recycled plastic bottles! It's amazing to think that the bottles can be melted down and changed into that lovely soft, snug material!

- A diamond is not just a pretty stone to put into jewellery. It is the hardest material in the world. It can cut through anything at all, even glass and rock. Many machines that are used for cutting and drilling use diamonds.

- Nylon is a man-made fibre, shown here, that is used in many clothes. It was invented by scientists working in both New York and London. They didn't know what to call this new material, so they took the letters of their cities and put them together: *New York LONdon*

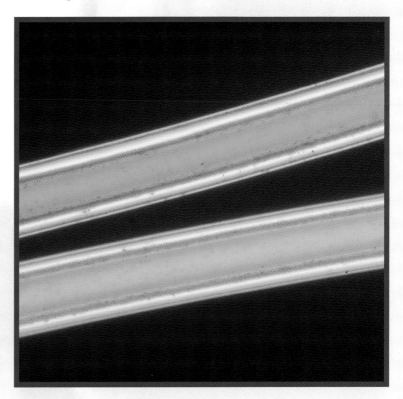

▶° Glossary

bleach chemical used to make a material become white or colourless

cavity hole in a solid object, such as a wall

conductor material that lets electricity pass through it. A heat conductor lets heat pass through it.

fabric material made of fibres woven together

fibre long, thin thread

flexible bendy

flexibility how much a material can bend

foam light, spongy material used for insulation and packing

humus pieces of dead plants and animals that are found in soil that has been broken down by micro-organisms

insulator material that does not let electricity pass through it. A heat insulator does not let heat pass through it.

manufactured make or produce in a mechanical way

material what something is made from

micro-organism very tiny living things that can only be seen with a microscope

mould formed into a required shape

nugget lump of pure gold

opaque cannot be seen through. A stone wall is opaque.

ore metal mixed with other things in the ground

property characteristic of a material. A property of stone is that it is strong.

rigid stiff and not bendy

sap fluid found inside a plant

sheared when the wool is cut off a sheep

transparency how see-through something is

transparent see-through. Glass in a window is transparent.